The CSS Alabama: The History of the Famous Confederate Raider that Sank Off the Coast of France during the Battle of Cherbourg

By Charles River Editors

Edouard Manet's painting of the Battle of Cherbourg

About Charles River Editors

Charles River Editors provides superior editing and original writing services across the digital publishing industry, with the expertise to create digital content for publishers across a vast range of subject matter. In addition to providing original digital content for third party publishers, we also republish civilization's greatest literary works, bringing them to new generations of readers via ebooks.

Sign up here to receive updates about free books as we publish them, and visit Our Kindle Author Page to browse today's free promotions and our most recently published Kindle titles.

About the Author

Sean McLachlan is an historian and archaeologist who specializes in the Trans-Mississippi Theater of the Civil War. He has written numerous books and articles on military history and is also the author of several works of fiction, including the Civil War novel _A Fine Likeness_ and the _Trench Raiders_ series World War One action novels. Feel free to visit him on his Amazon page and blog.

Introduction

An engraving of the Battle of Cherbourg

The CSS *Alabama*

"God helps those who help themselves." – The motto of the *Alabama*

After the first year of the Civil War, the Confederacy was faced with a serious problem. While the South had enjoyed some stunning victories on land, they had been all but cut off from the world at sea. The more industrialized North had realized that in case of an extended war, the best way to defeat the Confederacy was to starve it of supplies. The rebels started the war with no real navy to speak of, and so the federal government quickly set up a blockade of all Southern ports and river mouths. By depriving the South of revenues derived from its main export, cotton, the North seriously injured the Southern economy.

The South responded with a three-part strategy, but its best hope was in the diplomatic arena. Almost from the outset of the war, Confederate President Jefferson Davis had sent out agents to Europe in attempts to win recognition among major European powers, and to place even further pressure on the status quo, Southern merchants actually refused to export cotton, hoping the sheer weight of economics would compel them to help. As historian Charles Hubbard pointed out, "Davis left foreign policy to others in government and, rather than developing an aggressive diplomatic effort, tended to expect events to accomplish diplomatic objectives. The new president was committed to the notion that cotton would secure recognition and legitimacy from the powers of Europe. One of the Confederacy's strongest hopes at the time was the belief that the British, fearing a devastating impact on their textile mills, would recognize the Confederate States and break the Union blockade. The men Davis selected as secretary of state and emissaries to Europe were chosen for political and personal reasons – not for their diplomatic potential. This was due, in part, to the belief that cotton could accomplish the Confederate objectives with little help from Confederate diplomats."

Ultimately, this strategy, which lasted throughout the war, never bore fruit. Although the boarding of the RMS *Trent* by Union forces to take two Confederate diplomats off the British ship sparked an international crisis, in the end, none of the European powers had any interest in joining in the war, least of all the British. Their troops were all tied down controlling a massive empire that encircled the globe, and their venture capitalists soon discovered that cotton grew quite well in Egypt, which was already part of the British Empire. The loss of American cotton proved to be only a temporary inconvenience.

Without European intervention and the ability to build a navy that could rival the Union's, the Confederacy was mostly reduced to token resistance and using fast moving ships that could evade the blockade and import and export goods. Again, that was only partially successful, and today, the blockade runners are better known for their extracurricular activities; most notably, some of the crews also acted as privateers on the high seas, attacking U.S. shipping and taking any loot for themselves. The daring exploits of these commerce raiders caught the imagination of Southern soldiers and civilians and buoyed up morale, even as the war news turned increasingly grim.

Despite such impressive results, which fired the imaginations of Southern newspaper readers and gave them hope as the news on the battlefront grew increasingly bleak, the blockade runners were never able to adequately supply the Confederacy. Their shipments were too small, too infrequent, and too unreliable for a young nation on a war footing. By the last year of the war, blockade running had been all but strangled. Several major ports had fallen to the Union, and the rest were tightly blockaded. The blockade runners had also suffered from attrition. By the end of the war more than 1,100 of the ships had been captured and another 355 had been sunk or run aground.

Among all the Confederate commerce raiders, by far the most famous was the CSS *Alabama*. The *Alabama* attacked American ships and eluded the U.S. Navy around the globe for more than two years, all without ever having docked at a Southern port. The *Alabama* conducted seven expeditions, raiding commerce in locations as diverse as the Indian Ocean, Pacific Ocean, and Atlantic Ocean, capturing dozens of prizes across tens of thousands of miles of water. In fact, the

Alabama would meet its demise as a result of having to head into port in France to refit and repair the ship after so much heavy use.

While the Confederates tried to rely on blockade runners, the Union Navy assigned many ships the task of tracking them down and stopping them. One of these ships, the USS *Kearsarge*, would face off against the *Alabama* off the French coast. Unaware the Union ship was partly fitted with the armor of an ironclad, the Confederates decided to attack, and after the *Alabama* was escorted out of the French harbor by French ships, the *Alabama* and *Kearsage* dueled with each other in full view of hundreds of Frenchmen gathered on the coast. The battle lasted about an hour until the *Alabama* was headed to the bottom and dozens of its sailors were killed or wounded. Dozens more would be rescued, including some by the *Kearsarge*, and with that, the most famous Confederate raiding vessel of all was no more. The battle itself was celebrated in a number of artworks, including a few paintings by Edouard Manet, and the end of the *Alabama* brought relief to Union supporters across America.

The CSS Alabama: The History of the Famous Confederate Raider that Sank Off the Coast of France during the Battle of Cherbourg looks at one of the Civil War's most famous ships. Along with pictures of important people, places, and events, you will learn about the CSS *Alabama* like never before.

Chapter 1: Commissioning the CSS *Alabama*

In the wake of Abraham Lincoln's election in November 1860, Southern states began to gradually secede, and as the Confederacy continued to grow during his last months in office, President James Buchanan instructed the federal army to permit the Confederacy to take control of forts in its territory, hoping to avoid a war. Conveniently, this also allowed Southern forces to take control of important forts and land ahead of a potential war, which would make secession and/or a victory in a military conflict easier. Many Southern partisans within the federal government at the end of 1860 took advantage of these opportunities to help Southern states ahead of time.

One of the forts in the South was Fort Sumter, an important but undermanned and undersupplied fort in the harbor of Charleston, South Carolina. Buchanan attempted to resupply Fort Sumter in the first few months of 1861, but the attempt failed when Southern sympathizers in the harbor fired on the resupply ship.

In his Inauguration Speech, President Lincoln struck a moderate tone. Unlike most Inauguration Addresses, which are typically followed by balls and a "honeymoon" period, Lincoln's came amid a major political crisis. To reassure the South, he reiterated his belief in the legal status of slavery in the South, but that its expansion into the Western territories was to be restricted. He outlined the illegality of secession and refused to acknowledge the South's secession, and promised to continue to deliver U.S. mail in the seceded states. Most importantly, he pledged to not use force unless his obligation to protect Federal property was restricted: "In doing this there needs to be no bloodshed or violence, and there shall be none unless it be forced upon the national authority. The power confided to me will be used to hold, occupy, and posess the property and places belonging to the Government and to collect the duties and imposts; but beyond what may be necessary for these objects, there will be no invasion, no using of force against or among the people anywhere."

Lincoln had promised that it would not be the North that started a potential war, but he was also aware of the possibility of the South initiating conflict. After he was sworn in, Lincoln sent word to the Governor of South Carolina that he was sending ships to resupply Fort Sumter, to which the governor replied demanding that federal forces evacuate it.

Although he vowed not to fire the first shot, Lincoln was likely aware that his attempt to resupply Fort Sumter in Charleston Harbor would draw Southern fire, given that it had already happened under Buchanan's watch. After his inauguration, President Lincoln informed South Carolina governor Francis Pickens that he was sending supplies to the undermanned garrison at Fort Sumter. When Lincoln made clear that he would attempt to resupply the fort, Confederate President Jefferson Davis ordered General P.G.T. Beauregard to demand its surrender and prevent the resupplying of the garrison.

In early April, the ship Lincoln sent to resupply the fort was fired upon and turned around. On April 9, Confederate President Davis sent word to General Beauregard to demand the fort's evacuation. At the time, the federal garrison consisted of Major Robert Anderson, Beauregard's artillery instructor from West Point, and 76 troops.

At 4:30 a.m. on the morning of April 12, 1861, Beauregard ordered the first shots to be fired at Fort Sumter, effectively igniting the Civil War. After nearly 34 hours and thousands of rounds fired from 47 artillery guns and mortars ringing the harbor, on April 14, 1861, Major Robert Anderson surrendered Fort Sumter, marking the first Confederate victory. No casualties were suffered on either side during the dueling bombardments across Charleston Harbor, but, ironically, two Union soldiers were killed by an accidental explosion during the surrender ceremonies.

Beauregard

After the attack on Fort Sumter, support for both the northern and southern cause rose. Two days later, Lincoln issued a call-to-arms asking for 75,000 volunteers. That led to the secession of Virginia, Tennessee, North Carolina, and Arkansas, with the loyalty of border states like Kentucky, Maryland, and Missouri still somewhat up in the air. The large number of southern sympathizers in these states buoyed the Confederates' hopes that those too would soon join the South.

Despite the loss of Fort Sumter, the North expected a relatively quick victory. Their expectations weren't unrealistic, due to the Union's overwhelming economic advantages over the

South. At the start of the war, the Union had a population of over 22 million. The South had a population of 9 million, nearly 4 million of whom were slaves. Union states contained 90% of the manufacturing capacity of the country and 97% of the weapon manufacturing capacity. Union states also possessed over 70% of the total railroads in the pre-war United States at the start of the war, and the Union also controlled 80% of the shipbuilding capacity of the pre-war United States.

The Confederates would prove within months that they could hold their own on land, but the Union's naval superiority would never be questioned, and in fact, the potential for international recognition and intervention was the one way the Confederates could counteract the inevitable Union naval blockade. From the beginning of the Civil War, both the Union and Confederate governments knew that the United Kingdom could influence the outcome of the war, depending on whether or not it recognized the Confederate States and came in on its side. On the one hand, Britain's devout Queen Victoria and her even more devout husband, Prince Albert, opposed slavery and wanted to see it eradicated. On the other hand, the British mills desperately needed the cotton that only the Confederacy could fully supply. Lord Palmerston, then the Prime Minister of Great Britain, favored neutrality, as the nation had its hands full with European affairs, and he also maintained the British tradition of honoring other nations' blockades, again playing into the hands of the Union, which quickly and thoroughly blockaded Southern ports.

Queen Victoria

Lord Palmerston

At the same time, as far as the common people were concerned, the United States in any form was something to be disliked and distrusted. To understand this, it must be remembered that most adults living in England in 1860 had either lived through or had parents who lived through the War of 1812. Also, most had heard tales from parents and grandparents about the American Revolution, so to some degree, it may have seemed to many British that the United States was getting what it deserved. For example, on October 6, 1861, the *Saturday Review* ranted, "We do not agree with the *Times* in thinking that England stands in American opinion on the level of the least favored nation. We believe, on the contrary, that there is no nation whose esteem they so much desire; and that it is because they so much desire our esteem that they rail at us so much. The Americans crave for our sympathy, and, in a reasonable measure, they possess it. They have done their utmost to disgust and repel us. They have flourished in our faces manifestoes of buccaneering aggression. The statesmen and diplomatists by whom they have allowed themselves to be represented have exceeded in insolence, in ruffianism, in profligate dishonesty, all other statesmen and diplomatists with whom we have had to deal; and some natural exultation could not fail to be felt at the total break-down, in the face of real difficulties, of a set of low-bred swaggerers who had been 'chawing up creation' with their lies and their bluster, with their forged Oregon maps and their Monroe doctrines."

At the time the Civil War broke out, Charles Francis Adams, grandson of John Adams, was the United States Ambassador to the Court of Saint James, and he made it clear that the Union would consider Britain's recognition of the Confederacy to be an act of war. Adams had his work cut out for him even more because Britain did not particularly care for William Seward, Lincoln's Secretary of State. In fact, Lord Lyons, a British diplomat who knew Seward personally, once wrote, "I cannot help fearing that he will be a dangerous foreign minister. His view of the relations between the United States and Great Britain had always been that they are a good material to make political capital of...I do not think Mr. Seward would contemplate actually going to war with us, but he would be well disposed to play the old game of seeking popularity here by displaying violence toward us."

Lyons

Seward

Believing that England was ripe to be persuaded to come in on the Confederate side, in February 1861, two months before the attack on Fort Sumter, Southern President Jefferson Davis sent three diplomats to England to appeal for their help. The men were William Lowndes Yancey, Pierre Rost, and Ambrose Dudley Mann, and their instructions were to ""negotiate treaties of friendship, commerce, and navigation" with the British and the French. Their cause was bolstered by the fact that the British had long believed the United States was too big to survive and that is would inevitably split apart. Therefore, Lyons' instructions to his men was to try to broker some sort of peace agreement that would allow the Confederacy its independence without getting Britain involved in the fight.

In the end, foreign intervention would not be forthcoming. France and Britain were both busy maintaining their empires, and when the Confederacy actually stopped importing cotton to England in hopes of compelling the British to assist the South, the textile mills of Manchester and Liverpool found new supplies of cotton from Egypt and India. That said, during the first two years of the war, neither side in the Civil War was certain of Europe's intentions and whether a major power would play an active part in the war, so both paid close attention to foreign sentiment.

Regardless of how the Europeans acted, the Confederates also had to try to muster naval resources of their own, and in this regard, they were not terribly successful. The South lacked major shipyards and the industrial infrastructure with which to build a sufficient number of warships, so most of the ships that were launched were merchant vessels refitted for military purposes. Of course, many of these lacked the thick hulls and reinforced decks required for properly fighting a naval battle, even though a number of these ships did perform good service. A more serious problem was that they could never be produced in sufficient numbers to challenge the U.S. Navy. The Confederacy proved better at adapting its large supply of riverboats for fighting in the interior, where they fought Union riverboats throughout the war, but when New Orleans was captured in 1862 and Vicksburg was besieged and surrendered in July 1863, the Confederates lost all control of the Mississippi River, effectively cutting the Confederacy in two.

While Southern industry could never catch up with demand, especially as far as navies were concerned, the Confederates did manage to produce a remarkable number of warships considering the circumstances. The South even brought out ironclads and submarines, although as with the ocean-going vessels, their numbers were never enough.

Thus, the Confederates relied heavily on blockade runners. These ships, built more for speed than fighting, would slip past the Union blockade and trade with the rest of the world. Many of these blockade runners headed for nearby ports such as Nassau in the Bahamas, part of the British Empire, or to ports in Latin America. Others crossed the ocean and traded with Europe directly. They exported cotton and other Southern agricultural products and returned with weapons, gunpowder, and manufactured goods.

In the first year of the war, risks were low. It took time for the Union blockade to fully get in place, so a fast steamship under a bold captain stood a good chance of outrunning the blockading fleet and making it to the high seas, where it could lose itself in the vastness of the Atlantic or Caribbean.

Many of these blockade runners were painted gray to make themselves less visible at night. When sailing near land they often burned anthracite coal, which burns clean and thus reduces the chances of the ship being spotted from afar. Another clean-burning fuel was cotton soaked in turpentine, which burned so hot that it gave the engines extra power and speed. On the high seas, however, these expensive options were discarded and regular coal or sails were used. In those early days of oceangoing steamships, every vessel still retained a full complement of sails in case the engine broke down or the coal ran out.

The game of cat and mouse grew more serious as the war progressed. The Union fleet tightened its grip on southern ports and increased patrols along the Atlantic and Caribbean shipping lanes. Now only the fastest ships could make it through.

The main ports of call were various British possessions in the Caribbean such as Nassau and Bermuda, or the Spanish colony of Cuba. Here the blockade runners offloaded Southern goods, mainly cotton, which the British textile industry eagerly purchased despite the new cotton fields in Egypt, and traded for weapons, gunpowder, fuses, and percussion caps. A lively trade was conducted in other goods that were in short supply in the South such as paper and luxury items. Mail was also a vital shipment, since it was the only way the Confederacy, both its government and its private citizens, could keep in touch with the outside world.

The Caribbean route was a relatively short one. A good steamer could make it from Charleston to Nassau in 48 hours. The problem was that the Caribbean was relatively small and was soon swarming with Union vessels. If spotted, the blockade runner had to make a run for it. While the rebel ships carried guns, they were usually no match for a Union warship. Another tactic was to slip into the territorial waters of one of the European colonies. The Union pursuers did not want to breach the neutrality of these colonies and risk bringing in one of the major powers into the war on the side of the South, so once the blockade runner made it into British, Spanish, Dutch, or French colonial waters, it was safe until it had to leave, at which point it usually found the Union ship waiting.

Blockade running was a risky venture, but in the early years of the war it was one that was successful more often than not and brought vital supplies to the Confederacy. Perhaps the greatest run by one of these ships was done by *CSS Atlanta* when she brought 10,000 Enfield rifles, 1,000,000 cartridges, 2,000,000 percussion caps, 400 barrels of gunpowder, and a supply of swords, revolvers, and other military equipment into Savannah. That ship alone was enough to supply a small army.

Lieutenant Sinclair, who served on the *Alabama*, later noted how the circumstances of the war and the need for blockade runners produced the unique situation of requiring Confederate naval officers to gather abroad and attempt to build ships outside of the South:

> "The necessity of possessing a navy appealed very early to the government of the Confederacy, as was natural enough in view of the distress caused by the blockade, and the enormous advantages which Southern harbors and water-ways afforded to the enemy. But the South had no shipyards or machine-shops capable of building such vessels as were manifestly necessary to contend with the Northern armament. Only steam-vessels could effectively overhaul the swift Baltimore and New York clippers which carried Northern commerce, or manoeuvre against Yankee gunboats.

> "...A number of the most efficient naval officers of the South were therefore sent abroad to seek facilities not to be had at home, and to contract on the basis of the South's cotton-credit for such ships as were required...Capt. Jas. D. Bulloch, whose

brain conceived, and whose patience, caution, and executive ability, overcoming the most serious obstacles and discouragement, successfully materialized the 'Scourge of the Seas.' He arrived in Liverpool in the character of a private individual, and as such contracted with the Millers for the *Oreto* [later christened the *Florida*], and subsequently with the Lairds for the *290* (*Alabama*); Fraser, Trenholm, & Co., cotton merchants of Liverpool, assuming the responsibility of payment. The whole transaction was as between private parties, and so not liable to interference of the English authorities except upon proof of the violation of neutrality laws."

As a result, ironically, the most famous Confederate ship was not constructed in the South and would never dock in a Southern port. The *CSS Alabama* was commissioned and built at the famous shipyard of Birkenhead, opposite Liverpool, England. Many of the finest vessels on the high seas were built here by expert shipwrights working for the several large British companies based there. Sinclair described the ship:

"The *Alabama* was a screw steamer with full sail-power. She measured 235 ft. over all, beam 32 ft., tonnage 1,000. Her draft with full coal-bunkers was 15 ft. Her engines were two in number, horizontal, of 300 nominal, or 1,000 actual horse-power. She was barkentine-rigged, with very long lower masts, giving her principal sails an immense 'drop' or surface. She was at the same time a perfect steamer and a perfect sailing-vessel, each entirely independent of the other. Her screw, which was a two-bladed one, hoisted in a propeller-well, and when triced up was quite clear of the water, hence no drag or impediment to her speed under sail-power alone. Kept constantly under banked fires, and with frequent hoisting and lowering of screw, her crew and engineers executed this manoeuvre with surprising alacrity and precision. Indeed, so rapidly could she be changed from sail to steam-power that no enemy, appearing on the horizon in clear weather, could surprise her under sail, nor could a sailing-vessel of superior speed escape her before getting her full steam-power.

"The capacity of the coalbunkers was 375 tons, or sufficient for eighteen days full steaming. Her speed under the most favorable conditions was 13-4 to 13-6 knots by actual observation, or fifteen and three-quarters statute miles about the extreme of speed attained in sea-going vessels of that day. The armament consisted of one 8-inch solid shot or shell gun aft, one 7-inch 100-pounder rifle forward, six 32-pounders."

Deck scene, Cruiser Alabama

CAPE TOWN, AUGUST, 1863.

Lieutenants Armstrong and Sinclair; 32-pounder, Lieutenant Sinclair's division.

An image of Sinclair on the deck of the *Alabama* in his memoirs

A painting of the CSS *Alabama*

The best of the ship's eight guns was a 7-inch Blakely, a massive piece of firepower that launched a 100-pound projectile at an effective range of well over 2,000 yards. Unlike many guns of the time, it was rifled, not smoothbore, and thus had a greater accuracy, although it had a relatively short range compared to some other naval cannons. This piece was placed on the foredeck so that it could target ships that were trying to get away.

In all, the ship cost about $250,000 before it was launched on May 15, 1862. The ship had the innocuous name *290* and flew the British Union Jack. Since the British Empire was a neutral power, it would not allow warships for either the Union or Confederacy to be built on its soil, but as the name and the flag suggests, the rebels easily found a loophole. Building a merchant ship did not breach this neutrality, so the South ordered numerous ships to be built, had them launched as merchant vessels, and then subsequently fitted them with cannons and ammunition a different port. While it's altogether possible if not likely that they were aware of this ruse, the British shipbuilders ostensibly overlooked the fact that they were building a supposedly peaceful vessel with gun ports, reinforced decks strong enough to hold cannons, and a thick-walled powder magazine below the water line.

Thus, on July 29, 1862, the ship with the temporary name "hull number 290" went on a "practice run" from which it never returned. Instead of coming back to the British docks, the "merchant vessel" got past the USS *Tuscarora* before it could be intercepted and subsequently headed for the Azores, where she picked up her armaments and set out on her global adventure.

The USS *Tuscarora*

Tunis A.M. Craven, captain of the USS *Tuscarora*

Chapter 2: Captain, Officers, and Crew

Initially, the merchant vessel had a civilian crew, but this was all part of an arrangement by Confederate agents to bring the ship to a port where it would be given a true military crew. As captain, the Confederate government chose Raphael Semmes, and the 52 year-old Marylander proved the perfect choice for the job. Determined and resourceful, Semmes had experience with blockade runners from his time commanding the *CSS Sumter*, which in 1861 became one of the South's first commerce raiders.

Semmes

A picture of Semmes on the deck of the *Alabama*

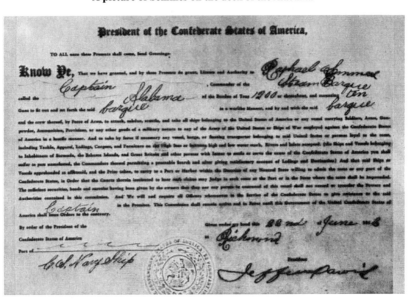

Semmes' commission to captain the *Alabama*

Semmes was a career naval officer, entering the U.S. Navy as a midshipman in 1826. He served during the Mexican-American War and made his home in Alabama. When that state seceded, he chose to throw in his lot with the South, and his first assignment was to command the CSS *Sumter*, a Spanish steamer originally called the *Habana* and later purchased by the Confederate government in April 1861 as part of the initial rush to procure boats for the embryonic Confederate States Navy. At the docks in New Orleans, Semmes oversaw her transformation into a warship that would serve both as a blockade runner and a commerce raider.

Photo # NH 54479   CSS Sumter running the blockade out of New Orleans, June 1861

RUNNING THE BLOCKADE.
(The Sumter and the Brooklyn.)

The *Sumter* running past the *Brooklyn*

The *Sumter* was commissioned on June 3 at New Orleans, and Semmes wasted no time breaching the blockade and getting to the high seas. She rushed past the *USS Brooklyn,* which had been tasked with stopping any ship coming out of the harbor, and eventually lost the Union ship in the open sea, freeing the *Sumter* to attack Union shipping. For the next six months, Semmes and his crew managed to sink or capture 18 American merchant vessels in the Caribbean, off the coast of Brazil, and later in the Mediterranean, all while constantly being chased by U.S. warships.

In January 1862, Semmes brought the ship into the port of Gibraltar at the mouth of the

Mediterranean Sea for a major overhaul, but the ship's boilers were found to be beyond repair. With that, Semmes and his crew left for England, later to be reassigned to the *Alabama*. This ensured that Semmes and many of the men who came with him on the new enterprise had valuable experience and knowledge that would serve them well in the years to come. Part of this was due to Semmes' strict discipline; indeed, the captain boasted in his memoirs that discipline was "never relaxed." Although "the willing and obedient were treated with humanity and kindness, the turbulent were jerked down, with a strong hand, and made submissive to discipline."

The officers for the new ship came from Nassau on a civilian steamer purportedly traveling on peaceful business. Semmes' second-in-command was First Lieutenant John McIntosh Kell, a 30 year-old career officer and a native of Georgia who resigned his commission with the U.S. Navy only an hour after his state seceded from the Union. His first assignment of the war was to command the paddle wheel steamer *Savannah*, a converted passenger vessel, and patrol the Georgia coast. When Semmes was given the command of the *Sumter*, he requested Kell be one of his officers, and he did this again when he was transferred to the *Alabama*. Kell was responsible for the day-to-day activities of the ship and also for discipline, which made him unpopular with many in the crew, although some later admitted that his harsh demeanor was necessary.

Kell

Kell on the *Alabama*

Kell and the other officers met with Semmes and the ship at the Azores. Then followed a long period of frenetic activity getting the ship into military shape before the rebel flag could be raised on her mast on August 24, 1862. At the flag raising ceremony, Semmes spoke with the crew, most of whom were Englishmen whose only task had been to deliver the ship to the Azores. At this point they were within their rights to ask leave to return home, but Semmes gave a rousing speech about the ship's true purpose, offering adventure and prize money to any man who stayed, along with double the wages they would make on a British vessel, paid in gold. A total of 85 did, leaving the *Alabama* about 20 men short, but it would be a simple enough affair to fill in the remaining vacancies from among the sailors who always lounged around any port looking for work.

One last detail remained before the ship was ready to start duty: she needed a motto. The one decided upon was *"Aide Toi, Et Dieu T'Aidera"* ("God helps those who help themselves"). This motto, inscribed on the brass rim of the massive ship's wheel, turned out to be all too appropriate because the *CSS Alabama* would pretty much be on her own for her entire run of service.

Chapter 3: Raiding Across the Atlantic

The *Alabama*, now fitted with guns and sufficiently crewed, sailed out to get into trim and give the crew a chance to familiarize themselves with the ship. While the officers and crew all had considerable experience, every ship has her own quirks and it takes time to adjust to sailing an unfamiliar vessel. However, they didn't have much time to practice, because less than two weeks at sea, on September 5, they spotted their first prize: an American whaling ship called the

Ocmulgee.

The *Alabama* approached under American colors, slipped alongside, and boarded her without a fight. It was only after the cheering rebels, many of whom had so recently been Englishmen, had leapt aboard brandishing their pistols and cutlasses that the whaling crew realized they had become part of the war. The whalers had just caught a sperm whale and had been in the process of stripping it of blubber and bone. The carcass of this unfortunate animal was discarded and the ship burned as her crew was kept on board the *Alabama* until they could be dropped off at a convenient port.

Lieutenant Arthur Sinclair, who was one of the original officers and stayed with the *Alabama* for her entire voyage, lovingly described how to burn a ship in his memoirs, noting that with all the whale grease smeared on a typical whaler, these were the easiest to burn: "First, you cut up with your broadaxe the cabin and forecastle bunks, generally of white pine lumber. You will find, doubtless, the mat tresses stuffed with straw, and in the cabin pantry part at least of a keg of butter and lard. Make a foundation of the splinters and straw, pour on top the lard and butter. One pile in cabin, the other in forecastle. Get your men in the boats, all but the incendiaries, and at the given word 'Fire!' shove off, and take it as truth, that before you have reached your own ship, the blaze is licking the topsails of the doomed ship."

Sinclair admitted to a feeling approaching shame at his first experience lighting up a vessel. A sailor naturally fears fire and never wants to see a ship burned, least of all by his own hand, but he and the rest of the crew soon became accustomed to it.

The next encounter was with the American schooner *Starlight*, which was both a transport and passenger vessel. The *Alabama* approached under a British flag and took the ship by surprise by firing a couple of shots across her bow. The skipper was inclined to flee to a nearby port in the Azores, but ultimately he decided against risking it because he had female passengers aboard.

After this capture, the *Alabama* preyed on the whaling fleet that operated in the seas around the Azores at that time of year, managing by October 1 to capture eight more ships, all whalers: the *Ocean Rover, Alert, Weathergauge, Altamaha, Ben Tucker, Courser, Virginia,* and *Elisha Dunbar*. These ships were all taken in a similar fashion - the *Alabama* would pull up close flying British or American colors, then fire a blank cartridge from one of her forward guns and hoist the Confederate flag. This generally brought quick acquiescence. Any ship that showed flight or resistance got a live shell across her bow, which usually made the ship come to a halt. Whalers had no weapons and couldn't match the *Alabama* for speed, so they generally surrendered at the first sign of trouble and were thus easy prey.

Little was taken from these ships except for items deemed necessary, such as clothing, spare tools, tobacco, and similar articles. Personal property was generally left untouched, but one item that was always taken was the chronometer, a valuable device and easily transported. The captured crew was often allowed to take their pick of the remaining items on board before the ship was torched. This gesture, which was easily enough given, helped breed goodwill and kept the prisoners from causing trouble.

In less than two months since her start of active service, the *Alabama* had managed to burn 10 American ships with a total value of about $230,000, almost the cost of building and outfitting the *Alabama* herself. This had earned her the attention of both the North and the South, not to mention the crews of all the neutral ships who had seen the conflagrations lighting up the Atlantic.

After clearing out the whaling fleet, the *Alabama* headed across the Atlantic to the Banks of Newfoundland, on the direct wind and water current between North America and Europe. It was here they hoped to catch bigger prey. The weather turned foul, but the crew continued to board any American vessels they came upon.

At this point in the war, there were few Confederate commerce raiders on the high seas, so most of these American merchant ships were undefended. By the 15th of October, the Confederates had taken seven more vessels: the *Brilliant, Wave Crest, Dunkirk, Manchester, Lamplighter, Emily Farnum,* and *Tonawanda.* Much of this constituted the so-called "grain fleet," which consisted of ships bringing American grain to the European market, so striking at these proved a more serious blow to the Northern economy than burning the whaling ships.

The *Alabama* next cruised well out from the east coast of the United States, hoping to intercept a troop transport headed south, but the search was fruitless and Semmes soon ordered the ship to head to the West Indies. On this trip, the only ships they caught was the *Levi Starbuck*, a whaler, which they fired, and the India clipper *T.B. Wales.* The latter ship proved to be a fortunate prize because the mainyard turned out to be the same dimensions as that of the *Alabama*, whose mainyard had been damaged in a storm. The crew took the mainyard for their own and was further surprised when 11 of the clipper's crew volunteered for duty on the *Alabama.* The new recruits were gratefully accepted on board.

By mid-November, the ship was off the island of Martinique, where on the 18th she met the CSS *Agrippina*, her supply ship. The two ships docked at Fort de France, Martinique, and the *Agrippina* transferred over to the *Alabama* a full load of coal.

While the Confederate commerce raider was moored at Fort de France, the U.S. Navy finally caught up with the *Alabama*. The steam frigate *USS San Jacinto* appeared outside the mouth of the harbor and waited for the rebel raider to come out. She was heavily armed with 12 guns and would have proven more than a match for the commerce raider and her crew, most of whom had never been in a fight. Fortunately for the *Alabama*, a dark and rainy night allowed the rebels to slip away.

The next goal was the east coast of Cuba, where the raider hoped to intercept a California mail steamer laden with a million dollars in gold. The steamer never appeared, so the crew had to content themselves with looting and burning the barque *Parker Cooke*. There followed several long days of finding nothing until early December when they came upon the steamer *Ariel*. The *Alabama* approached under American colors but the steamer sped away, perhaps suspecting the *Alabama* wasn't what she seemed. This grew to be a nagging problem for the commerce raider; the *Alabama* had used the trick of false colors too many times, and now when a captain saw a supposedly friendly ship come alongside to communicate, he suspected the worst.

Lieutenant Sinclair recalled the chase of the *Ariel:* "We had nothing left but to turn in pursuit, and in this manoeuvre some distance was lost. By the time her stern was presented to us she was a quarter of a mile ahead. There being no object in concealment now, our colors were changed. The *Alabama* had not as yet gotten the full benefit of her steam, and it was 'nip and tuck' between us, rather, if any difference, in favor of the enemy, who was now, we could see, doing her very best, her paddle-wheels turning with great rapidity, and dense smoke coming from the funnel. We could observe an immense crowd of passengers on her upper deck, principally women, interspersed with wearers of naval and military uniforms. Wishing to cut the matter short, Lieut. Armstrong is ordered to clear away the rifle pivot-gun of his division, and give her a shot above deck, taking care to strike her masts well above the passengers' heads. The *Alabama* is now yawed; and the sea being perfectly smooth, a careful sight is taken, lock string pulled, and in a moment splinters can be seen flying from the foremast about ten or twelve feet from the deck. Gallant shot! The mast is nearly cut in two, but holds on by the rigging. It was a great relief, you may be sure, to Armstrong that he had taken no life, particularly as the passengers were principally women and children. In a moment the ponderous wheels of the steamer cease to revolve, and she lay motionless on the water, completely at the mercy of the enemy. We came up with the prize fast enough now. Upon being boarded, she proved to be the California mail-boat *Ariel*, Capt. Jones, bound to the Isthmus, with a passenger-list of five hundred and thirty-two, mostly women and children, a battalion of United States marines under command of Capt. David Cohen, numbering, rank and file, one hundred and forty-five, and several naval officers, all bound to the Pacific station."

This capture proved to be more trouble than it was worth. Other than some money in the ship's safe and the soldiers' weapons, there was nothing worth taking from the ship and the large number of civilian passengers couldn't fit on the *Alabama*. Since it was against international law to tow a captured vessel into a neutral port, and there was no way to get all the people off so they could sink her, Semmes had no choice but to let the *Ariel* go. Meanwhile, the time it took to deal with all this allowed the California gold boat that they had been searching for to get out of the area.

The commerce raider then sailed up to the Gulf of Mexico and met with the supply boat *Agrippina* on December 23 and loaded up on coal once again. Supplying the ship with coal was a constant headache for Semmes and his officers, especially as they started to sail further from North America.

Next, the ship came off the coast of Galveston on January 11, 1863, to find the Union fleet shelling the city. When last the crew heard, the city had been in Yankee hands, but the shelling proved that the Texas land army had pushed the Union garrison out, and now the Union Navy was fighting to take it back.

This was part of a campaign by General Nathaniel Banks to take large portions of coastal Texas, in part to seal off the ports the blockade runners were using to supply the Confederacy. Semmes had been given orders to attack the troop transports that were part of this invasion, but what the crew of the *Alabama* didn't know until they arrived on the scene was that the Confederate riverboats and infantry had retaken Galveston, so instead of dealing with Union transports supplying a Union-held city, they instead had to deal with a Union fleet bombarding a Confederate city. As soon as the *Alabama* came into view, one ship from that fleet turned on her and the *Alabama* turned about and fled. The *Alabama* was flying British colors, but the Union Navy was taking no chances.

The chase lasted until after dark, at which point the pursuing ship came alongside and hailed the crew, and then asked them to identify themselves. Lt. Kell replied that she was a British ship called the *Petrel* and quietly gave the order to his gunners to fire on the word "Alabama." The pursuing ship, which turned out to be the *USS Hatteras*, announced they were going to send a rowboat over. When the boat was about halfway between the two ships, Lt. Kell shouted, "This is the Confederate States steamer *Alabama*!" Taking their cue to fire, the gun crews raked the *Hatteras* with a devastating broadside.

The *Hatteras* replied almost instantly, as her crew had been suspicious and had stayed close to their guns. The first broadside by the *Alabama*, however, was a deadly one, and so damaged the *Hatteras* that her gunners couldn't keep up a regular fire. After the *Alabama* had let off five more broadsides, there was the sound of an explosion from the engine of the Union ship, followed quickly by a call for surrender. The *Hatteras* was sinking.

Semmes dispatched boats to gather up the Union crew. While the Union ship had taken terrible damage, the crew of the *Hatteras* had only suffered two dead and five wounded. The *Alabama* had suffered only two men slightly wounded and little damage. The prisoners were paroled and dropped off at Port Royal in Kingston, Jamaica.

An illustration depicting the sinking of the *Hatteras*

Semmes' report on the fight against the *Hatteras* was full of praise for the crew: "My men handled their pieces with great spirit and commendable coolness, and the action was sharp and exciting while it lasted; which, however, was not very long, for in just thirteen minutes after firing the first gun, the enemy hoisted a light, and fired an off-gun, as a signal that he had been beaten. We at once withheld our fire, and such a cheer went up from the brazen throats of my fellows, as must have astonished even a Texan, if he had heard it." Semmes further reported that as far as his own ship was concerned, "there was not a shot-hole which it was necessary to plug, to enable us to continue our cruise; nor was there a rope to be spliced."

The *Alabama* stayed in Port Royal for a time to make repairs and restock, while the crew got to enjoy the town. Unfortunately, one of them enjoyed it too much. Paymaster Clarence Yonge got drunk with one of the paroled Union seamen and ended up speaking with the American consul in Kingstown. When Lt. Kell heard of this, he sent an armed party ashore, grabbed Yonge, and hauled him back to the *Alabama*, where he faced a court martial and had to leave the ship. Semmes would have been in his rights to hang him for treason, but he feared that this might hurt morale because Yonge had been a popular officer, and this popularity was proven when seven sailors didn't return from shore leave. How many of them deserted because of Yonge's influence, and how many simply followed the old sailor's tradition of getting so drunk that they missed their ship's departure, is unclear. Yonge later became a U.S. secret agent in London, spying on Confederate operations there.

Chapter 4: 1863

"It is two years to-day since we ran the blockade of the Mississippi in the Sumter ... Two years of almost constant excitement and anxiety, the usual excitement of battling with the sea and the weather and avoiding dangerous shoals and coasts, added to the excitement of the chase, the capture, the escape from the enemy, and the battle. And then there has been the government of my officers and crew, not always a pleasant task, for I have had some senseless and unruly spirits to deal with ... All these things have produced a constant tension of the nervous system, and the wear and tear of body in these two years would, no doubt, be quite obvious to my friends at home, could they see me on this 30th day of June, 1863." – Semmes, June 30, 1863

Semmes had to come to a decision as to what to do next. Despite the lucky fight with the *Hatteras*, he knew that going back to reengage with Banks' fleet would be risky, so he set course for Haiti to harry American shipping in that part of the Caribbean. That decision was quickly rewarded with the capture and burning of two ships carrying food, the *Golden Rule* and the *Chastelaine*. After this, Semmes set a course south for the coast of Brazil.

It is unclear why Semmes chose to go so far south. Perhaps he wanted to get out of the Caribbean and Gulf Coast area, which had become thick with American warships, and his subsequent decision to move across the Atlantic to the Cape of Good Hope suggests that he was already anticipating such a move. Semmes wrote in his log in January 1863, "This vessel had on board masts, spars, and a complete set of rigging for the U.S. brig Bainbridge, lately obliged to cut away her masts in a gale at Aspinwall [Panama]…I had tied up for a while longer, one of the enemy's gun-brigs, for want of an outfit. It must have been some months before the Bainbridge put to sea."

Whatever the case, he kept it from his officers, a habit he maintained through the *Alabama*'s career. Even his second-in-command Lt. Kell rarely knew where they were going next, but Lt. Sinclair had one theory for the southward move: "We had now been nine days out of port. Three vessels burned, but of insignificant value. We shall not make big hauls until the track of East India bound vessels is reached in Maury's 'road of the ocean,' a road all vessels must follow, cruisers or no cruisers. Navigators have only the choice of some sixty miles of width at one point off the Brazil coast. Neglect warning, stray from the mile-stones, and head or baffling winds and currents will waft you hither and thither, any way but the one wished. So here is the place for us to stand by, and also the place for Uncle Sam's cruisers to hold argument with us. It will therefore be understood why anticipation of another fight on our hands off the Brazilian coast makes much of the evening and mess talk."

Regardless, after several days of uneventful sailing, the *Alabama* had both good and bad action in early February. On February 2, the crew was concerned when fire broke out on the sihp, an event Semmes described: "The fire-bell in the night is sufficiently alarming to the landsman, but the cry of fire at sea imports a matter of life and death--especially in a ship of war, whose boats are always insufficient to carry off her crew, and whose magazine and shellrooms are filled with powder and the loaded missiles of death." Hours later, the ship captured and burned the merchantman *Palmetto* on February 3, 1863.

As the *Alabama* made it to this natural shipping route off the coast of Brazil, she captured a prize: the barque *Olive Jane* shipping from Bordeaux, France for New York with a hold full of wine, brandy, olives, and sardines. Lt. Sinclair was given the unenviable job of getting rid of the cargo of alcohol without the crew sneaking bottles off to their bunks. While the crew got two daily tots from the grog tub, any surreptitious drinking was bad for morale and work ethic and earned a severe punishment. Not wanting any trouble with the crew, Semmes ordered Sinclair to get rid of every bit of alcohol on the captured ship.

Sinclair realized there was no way to follow the order to the letter, so he followed it in spirit. Bringing up some of the choicest samples from the hold of the *Olive Jane*, he laid out a tempting meal complete with drinks in the captured ship's mess hall and invited the crew to tuck in. While they were thus distracted, the bulk of the liquor was destroyed and never made it aboard the *Alabama*.

Shortly after burning this ship, they captured the clipper *Golden Eagle* on February 21 and gave her similar treatment. Semmes reported, "I had overhauled her near the termination of a long voyage. She had sailed from San Francisco, in ballast, for Howland's Island, in the Pacific; a guano island of which some adventurous Yankees had taken possession. There she had taken in a cargo of guano, for Cork ... This ship [Golden Eagle] had buffeted the gales of the frozen latitudes of Cape Horn, threaded her pathway among its ice-bergs, been parched with the heats of the tropic, and drenched with the rains of the equator, to fall into the hands of her enemy, only a few hundred miles from her port. But such is the fortune of war. It seemed a pity, too, to destroy so large a cargo of a fertilizer, that would also have made fields stagger under a wealth of grain. But those fields would have been the fields of the enemy; or if it did not fertilize his fields, its sale would pour a stream of gold into his coffers; and it was my business upon the high seas, to cut off, or dry up this stream of gold ... how fond the Yankees had become of the qualifying adjective, 'golden,' as a prefix to the names of their ships. I had burned the Golden Rocket, the Golden Rule, and the Golden Eagle."

There was another lull as the ship experienced several times during her adventures. Any time she made a capture or two, the rest of the U.S. vessels cleared out of the area. News on the sea traveled amazingly fast, with ships running close by one another to exchange the latest information, and when a ship blazed up in the middle of the night, everyone within a radius of several miles knew a commerce raider was close by. It didn't take long for any American vessel in the area to find out and set a course at full speed for elsewhere.

At last the *Alabama* managed to capture and burn the *John A Parks* in early March, followed by a three-week lull before she captured and burned the whaling schooner *Kingfisher*. Throughout this time the crew was constantly boarding other vessels that turned out to be neutral. Any ship that was suspected of being a Yankee vessel, no matter what flag she flew, was boarded to check on her actual nationality. At times an American vessel would be boarded only for the crew to discover that it had been hired by some company of a neutral power to carrying goods that were neither going to nor coming from the United States. In these cases the ship was let go unharmed, for the Confederacy was at pains not to anger any of the European or Latin American powers. There was a vain hope throughout the war that some of these countries would come to the South's aid.

After another lull the crew's patience was rewarded by taking two American ships at the same time—the *Charles Hill* and the *Nora*. Semmes described the capture: "It was time now for the Alabama to move. Her main yard was swung to the full, sailors might have been seen running up aloft, like so many squirrels, who thought they saw 'nuts' ahead, and pretty soon, upon a given signal the top-gallant sails and royals might have been seen fluttering in the breeze, for a moment, and then extending themselves to their respective yard-arms. A whistle or two from the boatswain and his mates, and the trysail sheets are drawn aft and the Alabama has on those seven-league boots ... A stride or two, and the thing is done. First, the Charles Hill, of Boston, shortens sail, and runs up the 'old flag,' and then the Nora, of the same pious city, follows her example. They were both laden with salt, and both from Liverpool."

Besides adding two more sunken enemy ships to her register, the *Alabama* also gained nine crewmen, bringing her to a full complement of men for the first time in her voyage. The rebel sailors had gotten into the habit of trying to recruit men from the captured crews, and surprisingly this sometimes worked. Sailors considered themselves a breed apart, and not a few felt entirely neutral in the war that was ripping their country to pieces. Some had secessionist leanings, while others were simply attracted to the promise of good pay and prize money. Also, many crews had people from various nationalities and a large percentage of the *Alabama's* crew consisted of Englishmen.

An equally important prize came with the next capture, the *Louisa Hatch*, carrying a large cargo of high-quality coal. Semmes had been reluctant to dock in any port because the news would quickly spread about the raider's location. Staying on the high seas both made her safer and left the enemy ships in greater danger, so capturing this coal was just the thing to keep the *Alabama* in action and out of sight. Moreover, this was a special bit of good fortune because the *Alabama's* supply ship, the *Agrippina*, had not made their latest scheduled rendezvous. It wasn't until sometime later that Semmes discovered her captain had sold the supply of coal for his own profit. Needless to say, the thief never met up with the *Alabama* again.

The ship was now off the coast of Brazil and docked for a time at a Brazilian island port to rest and refit. While there, a sharp-eyed crewmember spotted two American ships nearby, the barque *Lafayette* and the brig *Kate Cory*, both whalers. The crewmen who happened to be on board and not on land hurried to their stations and after a long chase managed to grab both prizes, gaining another five volunteer sailors in the process. At this point, Semmes proudly boasted, "The fates seemed to have a grudge against these New England fishermen .... This was the sixteenth I had captured---a greater number than had been captured from the English by Commodore David

Porter, in his famous cruise in the Pacific, in the frigate Essex, during the War of 1812."

On April 22, the ship again sailed for the high seas, now with a full load of captured coal and a full mess of fresh food thanks to the Brazilians. Semmes and his officers were careful to make sure the men never took anything from the ships for themselves without prior approval. Any items taken from the ships was given to their respective departments. For example, any spare sailcloth went to the sailmaker, and items of general value were kept in common as part of the prize money. Often Semmes or Kell had to discipline sailors when they caught them stealing pipes or items of clothing from the prize ships. These items were unceremoniously tossed overboard and the sailor was docked a day's ration of grog. That punishment was considered enough for so slight an offense.

The hunting off the coast of Brazil turned out to be fruitful. The next ship they caught was the whaler *Nye*, which besides whale oil had a fine cargo of Virginia tobacco the crew enjoyed immensely. Then came the *Dorcas Prince*, followed by the *Union Jack* and the clipper *Sea Lark* at the same time, with the crew treated to the sight of a double conflagration. "Say what you will, we experience deep feelings of regret at this whole sale destruction of splendid ships and valuable cargoes," Sinclair wrote. "But as we peruse a batch of Northern newspapers, and learn of the devastation going on in our own dear land, we laugh at our mourning, with a heart steeled and embittered over again."

There followed another three-week lull until May 25, when they simultaneously captured the ships *Gilderslieve* and *Justina*. Then came the fine clipper ship *Jabez Snow*, a beautiful vessel that made the sailors wince when they torched her. Next came the barque *Amazonian* and then the clipper-ship *Talisman*, from which the crew got two 12-pounder brass guns and a good supply of powder and shot.

Another clipper, *Conrad*, fell into the rebels' hands shortly thereafter. Since she was such a fine ship, Semmes decided to outfit her with a skeleton crew and the two brass 12-pounders captured from the *Talisman* and use her as a commerce raider. She was renamed the *CSS Tuscaloosa* and on June 21, 1863, the ship was sent on her way.

It turned out that the new *CSS Tuscaloosa* didn't have much of a career. She sailed around fruitlessly looking for American ships, and when she later docked in Cape Town for refitting, the American consul complained that she was a captured American vessel and should be returned to her original owners. At first the British governor refused, but the consul insisted on taking the case to court, where his lawyers were able to convince the judge that since the ship had never been taken to a home port and condemned by a prize board, she couldn't be held by the Confederates in a neutral port. Semmes appealed the case and was able to convince the court of appeals that he was in the right, but by the time it made it through the legal system the war was all but over and the Confederacy had no way to claim her. The American consul and Captain Semmes had, in the end, both won the case and lost it.

After dispatching the *Tuscaloosa*, Semmes laid in a course along the trade winds to head across the southern Atlantic for the Cape of Good Hope, hoping to harass American shipping far from home (where it would prove easier pickings than it had already). Just before departing, the *Alabama* took one last American ship, the *Anna F. Schmidt*, loading up on a good supply of hardtack and boots and shoes, all needed for the long journey.

The ship set out and had good but uneventful sailing for several days before coming across the American clipper *Empress*, which she burned. The *Alabama* now had two captive crews on board and crowding had become a serious problem, but there was nothing to be done until they made landfall in South Africa. Their first port of call was Saldanha Bay on the west coast, a British possession about 60 miles from Cape Town. There they were able to offload their prisoners, stock up on fresh food, and make repairs after being battered by several storms in the long journey across the ocean.

Once this was done, Semmes ordered a course for Cape Town in order to meet with the British governor there and restock on coal. Throughout her globe-circling trip, the *Alabama* received warm hospitality from the British both at sea and on land. Numerous times, the captains of British ships offered to take prisoners off the crew's hands and act as mail couriers. They also gave valuable information about American warships nearby as well as newspapers that brought the rebel raiders up to date on the war effort back home. When at a British port, Semmes and his officers often dined with British officials and were the guests at balls and parties. The crew was given the run of the town. While the British Empire never joined the war on the side of the Confederacy, many British citizens felt sympathetic to the rebel cause. Whether this was a form of revenge for the War of 1812, or perhaps a calculated attempt to make the United States weaker by splitting it in half is a matter of conjecture.

On the short trip to Cape Town, the raiders got their first prize on the far side of the Atlantic, the *Sea Bride*, which was promptly boarded. It was sailing close to shore, however, and Semmes anticipated a protest from the American consul in Cape Town. Semmes judged the ship to have been captured six miles off shore, but knew the consul would disagree and claim it had been attacked in British waters, a breach of sovereignty that could create an international incident. Because of this, Semmes ordered the ship to be held, not burned. There followed a lengthy correspondence between the British governor, the American consul, and the captain of the *Alabama*. Both the consul and Semmes presented maps and compass bearings supporting their view, and the governor at Cape Town ended up asking various British sailors and lighthouse keepers who had witnessed the capture for their opinion. The British witnesses all said the ship was at least five or six miles out from land and thus in international waters. That settled the matter, and with that, the *Sea Bride* became a prize ship like so many other American ships that ran across the *Alabama*.

Even as the *Alabama*'s successes mounted, the Confederacy's hopes dwindled, and Semmes was incredibly discouraged by the news of Vicksburg's fall on July 4, 1863: "This [the surrender of Vicksburg] was a terrible blow to us. It not only lost us an army, but cut the Confederacy in two, by giving the enemy the command of the Mississippi River ... Vicksburg and Gettysburg mark an era in the war.... We need no better evidence of the shock which had been given to public confidence in the South, by those two disasters, than the simple fact, that our currency depreciated almost immediately a thousand per cent!"

Nonetheless, the *Alabama*'s quest continued, so after resting for a time at Cape Town, the *Alabama* rounded the Cape of Good Hope for the Indian Ocean and quickly made her first capture there—the *Martha Wenzell*. This time, she was hugging the coast close enough to be in British waters. This was a matter for debate, because she was five to eight miles from land, technically in international waters, but was inside the mouth of a large bay. The officers debated whether this meant she was in British territory or not, but since the matter seemed unclear Semmes reluctantly let her go. No one wanted to abuse the hospitality and good wishes of the British, especially after they had ruled in the raiders' favor in the *Sea Bride* case.

The *Alabama* was now on the popular trade route for the East Indies and stopped a steady succession of ships. They all turned out to be neutral, but it wasn't long before Semmes was given an offer to make himself and his crew some good money. A group of merchants approached him and offered to buy the *Sea Bride*, which the *Alabama* had not yet sunk. Semmes agreed, as long as the deal was done in international waters and away from the interference of the American consul. Soon the ship and all her cargo was sold for a hefty amount of gold totaling about one third of its total market value. This steep discount was due to the fact that the ship would have no nationality and thus no status, making her a bit of a risk for her new owners. Despite selling it at a bargain rate, this deal made the *Sea Bride* the most profitable of all the ships they captured. The merchants promised to buy any more ships that Semmes and his crew could deliver, and with the prospect of everyone becoming rich, the raiders sailed off in search of more prizes.

Unfortunately their run of bad luck continued as they found nothing but neutral vessels. The fruitless search continued until the middle of September, at which point a disappointed Semmes ordered the ship to round the Cape again and resupply the coal scuttles at Cape Town. From there she rounded the Cape yet again and headed to the East Indies.

The dry spell continued on the way there and for some time in the Indian Ocean until the middle of October, when the crew finally captured the American barque *Amanda* off the coast of Sumatra. Since the raiders were now more than 5,000 miles away from the merchants who had offered to buy their captured ships, Semmes ordered the ship burned. Supporting the Confederate war effort wouldn't be so profitable this time.

The next captured ship was the *Winged Racer*, full of a sugar cargo from Manila, which must have proven popular for the crew of the *Alabama*. Still, only two ships so far had been captured in the entire Indian Ocean, so Semmes steered a course for the South China Sea, hoping their luck would be better there. It proved a good plan, because on the way there, in the Gaspar Strait between the Indonesian islands Belitung and Bangka and connecting the Java Sea to the South China Sea, the raiders captured one of the most valuable prizes of her two-year voyage. This was the clipper *Contest*, the finest-made ship the officers and crew had ever seen. Many went on board to admire it before setting it on fire. Sinclair regretfully wrote that it was "a sacrilege, almost a desecration, to destroy so perfect a specimen of man's handiwork."

After this, the *Alabama* set sail through treacherous waters to make it to the South China Sea. Captain Semmes and his officers had to spend more than a week with practically no sleep, constantly studying charts for hidden shoals and keeping a sharp lookout during the daytime for reefs and other traps that would sink the ship as it made its way through a labyrinth of islands. These waters were also thick with Malay pirates who would quickly descend on any ship in trouble, so a wreck or beaching would mean death for everyone.

Progress was further slowed by the fact that Semmes didn't dare sail by night like he could on the high seas, and so each night the *Alabama* weighed anchor until dawn, when she could resume her slow, dangerous trip. This didn't offer Semmes a chance to rest because the nighttime hours were spent poring over charts and plotting the next day's course. What made the grueling journey worse was that not a single American vessel came into view.

The crew got a break from this exhausting routine when they stopped at the small French-owned island of Condore for refitting and took the opportunity to explore the jungle. Some of the sailors shot an ape, which the crew gathered around to examine. The main event, however, was shooting a vampire bat. This was passed around, still half alive and giving its captors an evil gleam and bared teeth. Everyone agreed it was the ugliest creature they had ever laid eyes on. The sailors had a completely opposite view of the local women, who went covered only in a breechclout and were eager to meet these strange men from across the sea.

As they got ready to leave Condore in December, Semmes figured something had to change: "The homeward trade of the enemy is now quite small, reduced, probably, to twenty or thirty ships per year, and these may easily evade us by taking the different passages to the Indian Ocean .... there is no cruising or chasing to be done here, successfully, or with safety to oneself without plenty of coal, and we can only rely upon coaling once in three months .... So I will try my luck around the Cape of Good Hope once more, thence to the coast of Brazil, and thence perhaps to Barbados for coal, and thence---? If the war be not ended, my ship will need to go into dock to have much of her copper replaced, now nearly destroyed by such constant cruising, and to have her boilers overhauled and repaired, and this can only be properly done in Europe."

The middle of December found them at the mouth of the Malacca Strait heading for Singapore with still no new prizes to show for their efforts. For the past couple of months, at nearly every port they visited, they had heard rumors that the American warship USS *Wyoming* was hunting for them. Captain Semmes and his officers closely questioned people who had seen her and knew that in a fight the *Alabama* would be seriously outgunned. The *Wyoming* did suffer from two disadvantages that gave the rebels some hope. The first was that she used up coal at a rapid rate and had to go to port more often than the *Alabama*. It was only her frequent absences from the chase that had kept her from finding the Confederate commerce raider by now. She also had large, vulnerable sidewheels. If the rebels could sail close enough in to use their guns and knock out these sidewheels, the *Wyoming* would be crippled. Getting into range without betting blown to splinters would be the challenge.

Each new rumor of this formidable Union vessel sparked long debates on board the *Alabama* as to who would win in a fight, and a fight there would certainly be if the two warships ever met up. There was no question of running from this challenge, because the Northern press had made out the captain and crew of the *Alabama* as cowards, willing enough to burn defenseless merchantmen but running at every hint that the *Wyoming* was drawing near.

However, there was no trace of her, and on Christmas Eve 1863, the *Alabama* left Singapore to head out once again through the Strait of Malacca for the long trip across the Indian Ocean. Once again they would face the perilous navigation of the South China Sea. The trip started out well that same day when the commerce raider captured an American vessel, its first in far too long. The ship was sailing under a British flag and with British papers that were seemingly in order. The bulk of her officers and crew, however, were American, and the skipper adamantly refused to speak with Semmes. The ship itself was also clearly of American make. This raised Semmes' suspicions, and he ordered her torched. This was risky, because if she did turn out to be British, the raiders would have alienated a potential international ally, but if she was an American vessel under false papers and was allowed to go, that would give a signal to all other American ships to try the same trick. Semmes took the risk and ordered her fired. As the ship went up in flames, the captured captain admitted that the ship was actually the *Texas Star*, hailing from Maine and sailing under false papers.

The next day, the crew got a Christmas present in the form of two American vessels, anchored and awaiting a fair wind. They had no chance of getting away and surrendered easily. They were the *Sonora* and the *Highlander*, both large clipper ships loaded with valuable cargos of rice. They may not have been capturing as many ships, but the crew was getting much better prizes than in the early days, when they settled for whaling boats around the Azores.

Chapter 5: The Battle of Cherbourg

"My ship is weary, too, as well as her commander, and will need a general overhauling by the time I can get her into dock. If my poor service shall be deemed of any importance in harrassing and weakening the enemy, and thus contributing to the independence of my beloved South, I shall be amply rewarded." - Semmes, February 1864

Off the coast of Ceylon in mid-January 1864, the *Alabama* took her next prize, the *Emma Jane*. Otherwise the trip through the Indian Ocean was quiet, with stops at islands to provision with tropical fruits and to meet the natives. There was also a magical night when they passed through some natural phosphorescence. Sinclair recalled, "I was keeping the first watch one night, and noticed about half past eight an appearance of milky whiteness in the sea ahead, as though in shoal water, accompanied by a brilliant phosphorescence. Although the chart indicated no shoal or land within hundreds of miles of us, still volcanic upheavals can occur in a day. The sight was so startling and sudden as to cause us to stand by for a grate on the rocks. The captain was called immediately, and the ship hove-to. Sounding with the deep-sea lead and getting no bottom at a great depth, our fears were allayed, and we filled away. A bucket of the water drawn showed innumerable bright particles sparkling and moving through it; but being kept for examination by daylight, it presented no unusual appearance. There was an unnatural light over the sea as far as the eye could reach, and to tell the truth it thoroughly alarmed every one. We thought the *Alabama* was to lay her bones in the Indian Ocean. We were several hours passing through it, showing it to be at least twenty-five or thirty miles in extent. The cause of this remarkable display of marine fireworks we could not determine, and even Semmes's experience was for once at fault."

This beautiful sight was followed sometime later by terrible lightning storms and high seas, which the *Alabama* was able to sail through relatively unharmed. In fact, she rarely suffered serious damage from any of the countless storms she passed through in her two year voyage, although the long ocean trips did work to wear down her fittings and require regular stops at port for minor repairs. Captain Semmes was scrupulous in keeping his ship in as good shape as possible, both for the practical purpose of keeping her battle ready and also because she was almost always the only representative of the Confederate States of America to dock in those distant ports. As such, she was a sort of ambassador and tool of international propaganda.

Even as the *Alabama* continued on its path, the whole world knew that the Civil War was turning against the South. The rebel army, which had once enjoyed a series of victories, was now constantly on the defensive and losing ground. Despite this, the *Alabama* enjoyed as friendly a welcome at Cape Town as it had on her previous visit. As the sailors strolled through the town and made visits to the nearby vineyards, they also kept an eye on the American gunboat and steamer *Kuang Tung*, which was also docked at Cape Town. She was headed to China to protect American interests amid the chaos of the Taiping Rebellion. There could have been no clearer message to the crew of the *Alabama* of how the war back home was going than that the United States Navy could spare a gunboat for service in far-off China when war was raging just south of the Potomac River and the nation's capital.

The two ships had spotted each other only after they had already sailed within British waters, so they made no hostile moves. On shore, the American and Confederate sailors avoided each other, which meant there were no barroom brawls to upset British neutrality.

The rebels also caught up with the international newspapers, which they hadn't seen for some time. All the war news was bad except for the effects of their own efforts. Article after article proclaimed the serious damage American shipping had suffered due to the commerce raiders. While the defeat of the Confederacy on land seemed inevitable, the men of the *Alabama* could console themselves in the thought that at least they had done their job well. Of course, they weren't the only ones; the *CSS Alabama* was only one of more than a thousand blockade runners and privateers operating for the Confederacy. Most were privately owned vessels operating under a letter of marque from the Confederate government. Their captains and crews were attracted by the rich prizes they could get by capturing Union ships, and also by the handsome profits to be made from trading with the outside world.

The *Alabama* left Cape Town in late March, having an uneventful journey up the west coast of Africa. Once the ship arrived in the vicinity of St. Helena, along the main current between Europe and the Americas, Captain Semmes ordered the sails furled. He decided to stay in the current for a time in the hopes of an American ship coming along. After a few days' wait, on April 22, 1864, the raiders get what they'd been looking for. The enemy ship tried to run and the chase lasted all night, with Semmes not pressing the matter because a nighttime boarding was more difficult and the prize wasn't fast enough to have a chance to get away. At dawn the next day, a single blank charge fired from one of the *Alabama's* forward cannons was enough to make her surrender. It turned out the ship was the *Rockingham*, carrying guano to Ireland, a less interesting cargo than some of the ones the raiders had captured but a valuable one nonetheless. Once the crew was taken aboard the commerce raider, the rebels used the *Rockingham* as target practice. What they couldn't know was that this practice would prove all too necessary.

A week later, while cruising westwards across the Atlantic, the raiders got their next prize, the clipper-ship *Tycoon*. True to her name, she was carrying a valuable cargo, which after being picked through was set on fire with the rest of the ship. The rebel raiders didn't realize it, but this was the last ship they would destroy.

Once they crossed the Atlantic, the raiders coasted up Brazil and found no enemy ships to board. Not wanting to get too close to the United States, where the Union navy was in full force, Captain Semmes decided to again cross the Atlantic. In May, he admitted, "The poor old Alabama was not now what she had been then. She was like the wearied fox-hound, limping back after a long chase .... Her commander, like herself, was well-nigh worn down. Vigils by night and by day, the storm and the drenching rain, the frequent rapid change of climate ... and the constant excitement of the chase and capture, had laid, in the three years of war he had been afloat, a load of a dozen years on his shoulders. The shadows of a sorrowful future, too, began to rest upon his spirit."

By June 10, the *Alabama* reached the English Channel, and the next day the boat docked at Cherbourg, France, for refitting. As *Alabama* sat in port in order to get repaired and refitted, the crew hoped to enjoy some shore leave, enlivened by a sampling of French wine. However, their holiday was cut short when the *USS Kearsarge,* under Captain John Winslow (who had literally fought alongside Semmes during the Mexican-American War), arrived three days later and stayed just outside the mouth of the bay, waiting for the rebel ship to show itself. The *Kearsarge* was a formidable vessel, a fine sloop-of-war with a low profile, good maneuverability, and seven guns.

Winslow

The *Kearsarge*

Manet's painting of the *Kearsarge*

Semmes soon learned of its presence, and through an intermediary he sent Captain Winslow a message on June 15 telling him that it was "my intention is to fight the *Kearsarge* as soon as I can make the necessary arrangements. I hope these will not detain me more than until tomorrow evening, or after to-morrow morning at furthest. I beg she will not depart before I am ready to go out."

What Semmes didn't know was that Captain Winslow had an ace up his sleeve. The year before, while docked in the Azores, he had secretly armored the *Kearsarge*. For a stretch of 30 feet on the midsection of the boat, both port and starboard, he hung thick iron chains as a makeshift armor. These he hid with an overlay of boards so that an enemy ship would not realize they were confronting a partial ironclad.

Even though he was unaware of this makeshift armor, First Officer Lt. Kell was reluctant to engage with the *Kearsarge*, which he knew had better guns than their own, including a pair of highly accurate 11-inch Dahlgren guns. He reminded Semmes that in target practice against the captured ship *Rockingham*, their gunpowder and fuses were of such bad quality that only one in three exploded. Semmes replied, "I'll take the chance of one in three."

It turned out Semmes was late for his appointment and did not sail out of Cherbourg until June 19. The *Kearsarge* was waiting. The log of the Union ship recorded, "At 10.20 discovered the *Alabama* steaming out from the port of Cherbourg, accompanied by a French iron-clad steamer, and a fore-and-aft rigged steamer showing the white English ensign and a yacht flag. Beat to general quarters and cleared the ship for action. Steamed ahead, standing offshore. At 10.50, being distant from the land about two leagues, altered our course, and approached the *Alabama*."

Captain Winslow had promised the French that he would not fight in French waters, and so the last-minute maneuvering was to make sure the ships were in international waters before the fighting began. Semmes, realizing what the Union captain was doing, also held his fire until he was sure both ships were out of French territory.

The French ironclad *La Gloire*, which escorted the *Alabama* into international waters

Once they had made it to international waters, Semmes was ready to fight. At a range of 1,800 yards, he ordered the *Alabama's* crew to open fire, but the shots went wild and Captain Winslow ordered his ship to head straight for the rebel vessel. His own guns lacked the range to fight at such a distance, so he needed to get closer.

The *Kearsarge's* surgeon, John Browne, wrote of what happened next:

"The action was now fairly begun. The *Alabama* changed from solid shot to shell and a shot from an early broadside of the *Kearsarge* carried away the spanker-gaff of the enemy, and caused his ensign to come down by the run. This incident was regarded as a favorable omen by the men, who cheered and went with increased confidence to their work. The fallen ensign reappeared at the mizzen. The *Alabama* returned to solid shot, and soon after fired both shot and shell to the end. The firing of the *Alabama* was rapid and wild, getting better near the close; that of the *Kearsarge* was deliberate, accurate, and almost from the beginning productive of dismay, destruction, and death. The *Kearsarge* gunners had been cautioned against firing without direct aim, and had been advised to point the heavy guns below rather than above the water-line, and to clear the deck of the enemy with the lighter ones. Though subjected to an incessant storm of shot and shell, they kept their stations and obeyed instructions.

"The effect upon the enemy was readily perceived, and nothing could restrain the enthusiasm of our men. Cheer succeeded cheer; caps were thrown in the air or overboard; jackets were discarded; sanguine of victory, the men were shouting, as each projectile took effect: 'That is a good one!' 'Down, boys!' 'Give her another like the last!' 'Now we have her!' and so on, cheering and shouting to the end."

Semmes, too, decided to get closer. His long-range guns weren't hitting, and his big gun, the 7-inch Blakely, had a relatively short range. He later recalled that he "wished to get within easy range of his enemy, that he might try this weapon effectively; but any attempt on his part to come to closer quarters was construed by the *Kearsarge* as a design to bring the engagement between the ships to a hand-to-hand conflict between the men. Having the speed, she chose her distance, and made all thought of boarding hopeless."

Without the ability to board, the two ships continued to circle each other in the water, with the *Alabama*'s shots barely causing damage against the iron plating of the *Kearsarge*. Winslow's tactic turned out to be all the more wise because it was a long distance shot from the *Alabama*'s Blakely gun that made the only good hit on the Union ship in the entire fight. As Surgeon Browne wrote after the war, "After the *Kearsarge* had been exposed to an uninterrupted cannonade for eighteen minutes, a 8-pounder [sic] Blakely shell passed through the starboard bulwarks below the main rigging, exploded upon the quarter-deck, and wounded three of the crew of the after pivot-gun. With these exceptions, not an officer or man received serious injury. The three unfortunate men were speedily taken below, and so quietly was the act done that at the termination of the fight a large number of the men were unaware that any of their comrades were wounded. Two shots entered the ports occupied by the thirty-twos, where several men were stationed, one taking effect in the hammock-netting, the other going through the opposite port, yet none were hit. A shell exploded in the hammock-netting and set the ship on fire; the alarm calling for fire-quarters was sounded, and men who had been detailed for such an emergency put out the fire, while the rest staid at the guns." One of the injured men would later die of his wounds. He was the only Union fatality in the fight.

Meanwhile, the Union gunfire was taking a much heavier toll, as Captain Semmes wrote in his official report:

> "The firing now became very hot and the enemy's shot and shell soon began to tell upon our hull, knocking down, killing, and disabling a number of men in different parts of the ship.

> "Perceiving that our shell, though apparently exploding against the enemy's sides, were doing but little damage, I returned to solid shot firing, and from this time onward alternated with shot and shell. After the lapse of about one hour and ten minutes our ship was ascertained to be in a sinking condition, the enemy's shell having exploded in our sides and between decks, opening large apertures, through which the water rushed with great rapidity."

The fatal shot came from one of the *Kearsarge's* Dahlgren guns. The shell hit the starboard right at the waterline and punched a large hole right through it. Water rushed in and the ship began to sink. Semmes recalled, "After the lapse of about one hour and ten minutes, our ship was ascertained to be in a sinking condition, the enemy's shells having exploded in our side, and between decks, opening large apertures through which the water rushed with great rapidity. For some minutes I had hopes of being able to reach the French coast, for which purpose I gave the ship all steam, and set such of the fore and aft sails as were available. The ship filled so rapidly, however, that before we had made much progress, the fires were extinguished in the furnaces, and we were evidently on the point of sinking. I now hauled down my colors to prevent the further destruction of life, and dispatched a boat to inform the enemy of our condition."

This wasn't enough to stop the fight, however. The *Alabama's* gun ports were still open, and some witnesses report that a couple of her guns fired after the flag had been run down. Thus, Captain Winslow ordered his gunners to continue firing. One of these witnesses was Surgeon Browne, who wrote, "Captain Winslow, amazed at this extraordinary conduct of the enemy who had hauled down his flag in token of surrender, exclaimed, 'He is playing us a trick; give him another broadside.' Again the shot and shell went crashing through her sides, and the *Alabama* continued to settle by the stern. The *Kearsarge* was laid across her bows for raking, and in position to use grape and canister."

Soonafter, a crewmember on the *Alabama* waved a white flag and the firing stopped for good. All told, the *Kearsarge* had fired about 175 shots and the *Alabama* nearly 350, but only about 30 of the *Alabama*'s connected. As he ordered his crew to save themselves however they could, Captain Semmes threw his sword into the sea rather than have to suffer the dishonor of handing it over to Captain Winslow.

For a few minutes the Union ship held off, worried about another trick, and then sent boats to pick up the crew. They weren't the only ones. The English yacht *Deerhound*, which had been sailing close by to watch the fight, retrieved 41 of the crew along with Semmes and First Officer John Kell. They returned to Cherbourg, where one of the wounded crewmembers died. The remainder later shipped to England, where they were feted as heroes and Semmes wrote that he was presented with "a magnificent sword, which had been manufactured to their order in London, with suitable naval and Southern devices." Nonetheless, it must have been a bittersweet celebration, however; the crew of the *Alabama* had lost 26 dead and 21 wounded. Semmes concluded his report by saying, "My officers and men behaved steadily and gallantly, and though they have lost their ship they have not lost honor."

Winslow's tracking map of the battle

A lithograph depicting the battle

A picture of a cannonball lodged in the sternpost of the *Kearsarge*

A depiction of the surrender of the *Alabama*

Harper's Weekly engraving of the sinking of the *Alabama*

Pictures of the deck of the *Kearsarge* after the battle

After the Battle of Cherbourg, Semmes assumed he was done fighting, writing, "I considered my career upon the high seas closed by the loss of my ship, and had so informed Commodore Barron, who was our Chief of Bureau in Paris." However, he was wrong, and the sinking of the *Alabama* didn't take the fight out of those of her crew who escaped. Those who had managed to get to France eventually made their way back to the Confederacy, sailing first to Cuba and then sneaking through the blockade to Texas. From there, Semmes, Kell, and the sailors had a long trek across the Confederacy to Richmond, Virginia. There, in February of 1865, Semmes was promoted to rear admiral.

Of course, by this point there wasn't much of a Confederate Navy to speak of. Semmes and Kell were assigned to the James River Squadron, a modest collection of riverboats tasked with defending the capital. Kell was made captain of the ironclad *CSS Richmond*, while Semmes was given overall command of the fleet, but this arrangement lasted only a few weeks. The Confederate capital fell on April 3, and Admiral Semmes ordered the James River Squadron burned to keep it from falling into the hands of the Union army.

After that, the crews took up infantry weapons, reformed as the Naval Brigade, and tried to retreat with General Robert E. Lee's Army of Northern Virginia. Only a few made it, with the rest under Semmes being cut off and forced to retreat to the south, where they joined with General Joseph Johnston's forces. Johnston made Semmes a brigadier general, putting Semmes in the unique position of being both a general and an admiral.

The war was coming to an end, however. Lee surrendered the Army of Northern Virginia to Ulysses S. Grant at Appomattox Court House on April 9, and Johnston, understanding that the war was at an end, arranged to surrender to William Tecumseh Sherman at Bennett Place, North Carolina, on April 26. Semmes and his Naval Brigade surrendered with the army and spent three months in jail before being released.

Upon his release, Semmes soon took up practicing law, while Kell became a farmer in Georgia. The rest of the officers and crew also turned towards more peaceful pursuits, always remembering their glory years on the high seas. Semmes would write after the war, "Whatever else may be said of me, I have, at least, brought no discredit upon the American name and character."

In retrospect, the adventure of the *CSS Alabama* was not a great assistance to the Confederate war effort. It did not lend its support in any major campaigns or sink any important naval vessels. It did, however, amass an impressive record of 65 sinkings or captures, better than any other Confederate commerce raider. Historians estimate that it cost American merchant shipping more than $4.5 million in losses, a huge amount at that time, and Sinclair put the estimate at $6.75 million. As a matter of comparison, a private in the U.S. Army was paid $13 a month.

That said, while the *Alabama* did strike a series of pinpricks to the Northern maritime economy, its use was far more as a morale boost than as an actual weapon of war. Like with the blockade runners and commerce raiders in general, while the *CSS Alabama* struck a blow for the Southern cause, it could not change the outcome of the war. It was more of a propaganda coup for the South and an annoyance to the North, but its incredible exploits around the globe, travelling some 75,000 miles (the equivalent of three times around the Earth) earned it a place in Civil War lore and won the ship and its crew a place in naval history.

In the 1980s, underwater archaeologists discovered the wreck of the *CSS Alabama* and conducted a partial excavation. Despite excavating in difficult conditions under 178 feet of water and with a four-knot current, they retrieved numerous artifacts, including Captain Semmes' toilet bowl, a white porcelain commode decorated with a country scene in blue. Also found were the brass rim of the ship's wheel inscribed with the ship's motto (the wood of the wheel itself had rotted away). Other recovered artifacts included the copper chimney used in the galley, a cannonball, and several pieces of crockery.

A later addition to the collection was the ship's bell, which was suspected to have been stolen from the site and later recovered by police from an antiquities dealer in New Jersey. Theft of artifacts, both on land and at sea, is a constant problem at archaeological sites of all periods, especially famous Civil War sites. The dealer objected that the *Alabama* was a pirate ship and therefore not legally protected, a creative but poor line of reasoning. There was also the question, still unresolved, of whether the bell came from the ship at all. The engraving on the bell is rather crude, which inconsistent with the fine quality of the artifacts known to have come from the ship, and naval experts believe it's too small for a ship of that size.

Regardless of its status, the bell and the other artifacts remain a telling reminder of the legendary voyage of the Confederate commerce raiders.

Online Resources

Other Civil War titles by Charles River Editors

Other books about 19th century American history by Charles River Editors

Other books about the CSS Alabama on Amazon

Bibliography

Bowcock, Andrew. *CSS Alabama, Anatomy of a Confederate Raider*. London, United Kingdom: Chatham Publishing, 2002.

Delaney, Norman C. "John McIntosh Kell, 'Luff' of the *CSS Alabama*" in *The Confederate Naval Historical Society Newsletter*. Confederate Naval Historical Society: Issue Number Nine, February 1992.

Hearn, Chester G., *Gray Raiders of the Sea*. Baton Rouge, LA: Louisiana State Press, 1996.

Luraghi, Raimondo. *A History of the Confederate Navy*. Annapolis, MD: U. S. Naval Institute Press, 1996.

Semmes, Raphael, Admiral, CSN. *Memoirs of Service Afloat During the War Between the States*. Fredericksburg, VA: Blue & Grey Press, 1987.

Semmes, Raphael, Admiral, CSN. *The Cruise of the Alabama and the Sumter*. New York City, NY: Carleton, 1864.

Sinclair, Arthur, Lieutenant C.S.N. *Two Years on the Alabama*. Boston, MA: Lee and Shepard Publishers, 1896.

Townley, John. "C.S.S. Alabama Artifacts Exhibit at U.S. Naval Museum opens with All-Star Franco-American Reception" in *The Confederate Naval Historical Society Newsletter*. Confederate Naval Historical Society: Issue Number Nine, February 1992.

United States Naval War Records Department. *Official Records of the Union and Confederate Navies in the War of the Rebellion.* Washington, D.C.: Government Printing Office, 1922.

United States War Department. *The War of the Rebellion: A Compilation of the Official Records of the Union and Confederate Armies.* Washington, D.C.: Government Printing Office, 1888.

Made in United States
North Haven, CT
01 November 2022

26181050R00033